CHEERLEADING AND
BATON TWIRLING

CHEER-LEADING AND BATON TWIRLING

BY SHAN FINNEY
Illustrations and diagrams
by the author

Franklin Watts
New York|London|Sydney|Toronto|1982
A First Book

Library of Congress Cataloging in Publication Data

Finney, Shan.
Cheerleading and baton twirling.

(A First book)
Includes index.
Summary: Contains illustrated instructions for
basic cheerleading and baton twirling routines
including yells, jumps, and twirls.
1. Cheerleading—Juvenile literature. 2. Baton
twirling—Juvenile literature. [1. Cheerleading.
2. Baton twirling] I. Title.
LB3635.F56   791'.64   81-22009
ISBN 0-531-04391-6   AACR2

Contents

PART II · BATON TWIRLING

Thanks to
Liz Oatell and
Yvette Thor

Small Beginnings

Can you imagine a football game without cheerleaders or a band without twirlers? Probably not! But both cheerleading and baton twirling are newer than you might think. It is only in the last thirty years that they have become skilled, organized activities.

Cheerleading grew out of the wild yells of enthusiastic crowds. Twirling began with the baton majors who beat time at the head of marching bands. Over the years both activities have grown up little by little. And they are still growing!

This means that there is still room for you to learn and grow with them. Today's complicated routines came from small beginnings. You can learn them the same way that they grew —bit by bit.

First, you must learn the basic movements. These are the parts from which cheering and twirling routines are built. Learning them will sometimes feel like very hard work. But with practice you will soon be able to do the basics. Then you can put them together to build your own routines. Before you know it you will be ready to invent moves of your own.

PART I

CHEERLEADING

Chapter 1:
Leadership and Spirit

Cheerleading is fun. It is an exciting way to show off your personality and talent. But it is also work. Those lively people along the sidelines at the game have two very important jobs.

First, cheerleaders keep up the spirit of their school or club. They cheer the team to win. Just as important, they boost spirit even when the team is losing. Second, cheerleaders set an example for the crowd. To do this you must be a good sport. Everything you do in front of the crowd must be in good taste. Sometimes the crowd may become disappointed or angry. Then you must lead them in cheers that show them how to be good sports.

As a cheerleader you will develop some valuable skills. You will have the opportunity to practice good judgment, spirit, and poise. Your strong, energetic personality will be in the spotlight.

Chapter 2:
Getting Ready

As you begin to practice cheerleading, here are a few things to keep in mind.

WHAT TO WEAR

When you practice always wear comfortable clothing. Your arms, legs, and body must go through all sorts of twists, turns, and jumps. If your clothes are too tight, your movements will be, too. Floppy skirts or baggy pants are not any better. They wrap around your legs or block your movements. Never wear clothes that bind or get in your way.

For both boys and girls, T-shirts and shorts make good practice outfits. In cool weather, change them for sweatshirts and loose slacks. Wear tennis shoes to keep your feet light and give them a firm grip. Avoid shoes with thick or stiff soles.

WHERE TO PRACTICE

To practice you will have to jump and yell. Make sure you have plenty of room. A *side banana* jump that ends against a brick wall might make you a squashed banana.

You must also make sure that your yells and stomps do not disturb other people. A big, grassy yard is a good place to practice. If you do not have a yard, go to a park or school near your home.

WARM-UPS
A cheerleader needs a limber body. To avoid strained muscles, always do at least fifteen minutes of warm-ups before you practice. Here are a couple of exercises to try:

LEG STRETCHES: Sit on the floor, with your legs straight and your feet apart. Bend your left knee. Rest your left foot against the upper part of your right leg. Keep your right leg straight. Point your toes forward. Bend at the waist and stretch both arms toward your right foot. Then straighten your waist. Point your toes toward your body and stretch again. Now bend your right leg and straighten your left. Repeat the stretches.

SIDE BENDS: Stand straight. Stretch both arms straight out to your sides, shoulder high. Bend to the right as far as you can. Return to starting position. Bend to the left. Repeat the bends to the right and left.

VOICE

To lead cheers, you must also have a good voice. With practice, you can make your voice stronger and clearer.

First, put one hand on your stomach. Now talk. Yell "Okay, let's go." Your stomach muscles should move. Can you feel them tighten?

To make your words clearer, say the letters of the alphabet out loud. Shape each sound with your lips. Place one hand on your stomach while you do it. Make your words start in your stomach. Shape them with your lips as they leave your mouth. Now you are ready to begin!

Chapter 3:
Beginnings

Each cheer has three main parts. The parts are the *beginning*, the *yell*, and the *ending*. The yell is the biggest part of the cheer. The beginning leads straight into the yell. The ending comes right after the yell. When a cheer is performed, all three of its parts must flow together smoothly. No one notices that they are really separate units. But they are, and that is half the fun! You can mix and match the parts any way you want.

The beginning of a cheer does two important things. First, the beginning tells the crowd you are ready to start the cheer. It gets everyone's attention before you go into the yell itself. Second, a beginning sets the beat for the cheerleaders. It helps get everyone off on the same foot.

Here are five beginnings. Learn them step by step. When you know where to move your arms and legs, work on your style. Make the short movements quick and lively. The long movements should be wide and smooth. Remember to let your personality show. Your enthusiasm is as important as getting the steps right!

ARM THRUST

This is an easy beginning to start out with. Later you can use the same movements as part of a yell. For now, do them to a count of one-two-three. One—thrust both arms straight up above your shoulders. Two—bring your hands back down to your shoulders. Three—thrust both arms straight out to your sides. Make your hands into fists. Put some punch behind them!

FINGER SNAP

The Finger Snap has three steps. Stand straight with your feet together. Put your hands on your hips. Now do the first three motions all at the same time. Thrust your hands out to your sides. Snap your fingers. Put your right foot forward. Your heel is on the ground and your toes point up. Second, swing your arms back in to your sides. Snap your fingers as you move your arms. Third, bring your foot back to starting position. Do it with one quick, firm step. Now clap your hands quickly three times.

SNAP FOUR

This time you will snap your fingers to four different motions. Keep your hands waist high. Snap your fingers as you move your arms. With elbows bent, cross your right arm in front of your waist. At the same time, cross your left arm in back. Snap one. Now move your arms back to your sides. Snap two. Next cross your left arm in front and your right arm in back. Snap three. Move your arms back to your sides again. That is snap four! End up with hand claps. Clap twice; skip a beat; clap twice again.

1   2   3   4

SALUTE

To start the Salute, stand straight. Put your feet together and your arms at your sides. Make a fist with your right hand. Raise your right arm, elbow bent. Touch the back of your fist to your forehead. Now fling your right arm straight out to your side. At the same time step to the right with your right foot.

1

2

3

WAIST TWIST

Again stand straight with your feet together. Put your hands on your hips. Now throw your arms out to your sides at shoulder height. At the same time kick your left leg across in front of your right leg. Keep your left leg straight and kick as high as you can. At the top of the kick, swing your left leg far to the left. When your left foot hits the ground, your feet will be wide apart. Your arms are still out to your sides. Now arch your body to the left. Put your weight on your left foot. Bend your right knee. Spring off your left foot and leap to your right. Start the yell as you leap.

WORDS AND COUNTS,
SNAPS AND CLAPS

You have already used hand claps and finger snaps with other movements. For a simple beginning, you can use snaps and claps alone. Clap your hands as you work out the rhythm of a yell. Then clap in the same rhythm to begin the yell.

Words alone can be used for beginnings. Here are four beginning lines.

> Okay, let's go.
> All set, you bet.
> Are you ready? Let's go.
> Okay, take it away!

Try yelling them to different rhythms. Say "O-*kay*, let's *go*." Clap as you say it. Clap, *clap*—clap, *clap*. Now say "o-kay-let's-go." Say it to a clap-clap-clap-clap. Work out your own rhythms for the other lines.

You can also begin with counts. A count is simply a series of numbers. In the Arm Thrust, you used a count of one-two-three. Yell the numbers alone. Yell them along with movements. Mix them with snaps and claps.

Words and movements are the bits that make up cheers. The more ways you mix them, the more interesting your cheers will be.

WHEN NOT TO BEGIN

All cheerleaders should know when *not* to cheer. A cheer must never get in the way of the game, the team, the coach, or the crowd. Do not cheer in the active playing area. Leave the floor when the game is about to start. When the team is in a huddle, do not cheer too close to them. And never block the crowd's view of the game. Put your own good sense to work. Remember, good judgment is part of your job as a cheerleader!

— 15 —

Chapter 4: Movements

The yell is a set of words that cheerleaders match to movements. It is the biggest part of the cheer. Every yell can be done many different ways. Cheerleaders at different schools often yell the same words. But they usually work out their own movements. To do this, you must learn a variety of movements.

When you did beginnings, you used hand positions, arm movements, and footwork. These are the three kinds of movements you mix and match to build cheers. Learn some of each. Then you will learn words to yell with them.

HAND POSITIONS

Fists are just what they sound like. They go with arm movements that thrust, punch, or pull.

Blades go with sharp, slicing movements. To make blades, hold your fingers together straight out and stiff.

Fans are just like blades, except that your fingers are spread wide apart. Fans look good with wide, sweeping arm movements.

For *cups*, your hands are cupped as though you were dipping water. Your fingers are close together and curved. Cups go with short, choppy arm movements.

Practice all four hand positions and learn their names. Try different hand positions with the beginnings you learned earlier.

ARM MOVEMENTS
Cheerleading movements must be easy to see from a distance. Make your arm movements wide and smooth, or quick and sharp. When your arms are straight, keep them stiff. Lock your wrists and elbows. Reach out or up as far as you can. When you curve your arms, stretch as though you are shaping big circles. Try to make the circles bigger each time.

SWEEPS: Sweeps go with the fan hand position. Use this starting position for all sweeps. Stand with your arms straight down at your sides, elbows locked. Lift your arms about twelve inches out from your sides. Turn your palms forward. Shape your hands into fans. Now you are ready to start.

To do an *overhead sweep*, shape a big circle with both hands. Lift both arms out from your sides and up. Raise your arms until your hands meet above your head. Now draw the same circle backward. You are back to starting position.

Start the *chest sweep* the same way you started the over-head. As your hands meet above your head, let them cross. Move your crossed hands downward in front of your face and chest. Draw the same shape backward to return to starting position.

Now try an *inside-out sweep*. Point your fingertips upward. Turn your palms forward. To do this you will have to bend your wrists and elbows. Now move your hands toward each other. When they cross, move them upward. When both hands are straight above your head, move them apart. Stop when your hands are straight out to your sides and slightly higher than your shoulders. Do the same movements in reverse.

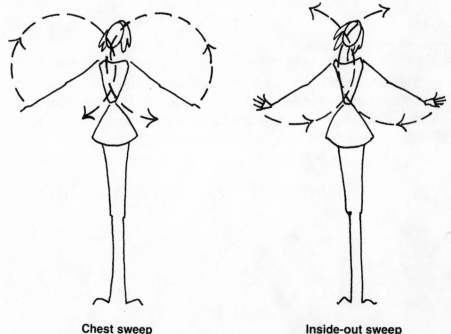

Chest sweep   **Inside-out sweep**

SLICES AND CHOPS: To slice, imagine that a ribbon is stretched tight in front of you. Make your hands into blades. Bend your elbows and raise your hands up to your shoulders. Your palms should face each other. Slice your hands down through the imaginary ribbon. Your hands keep moving after they cut the ribbon. A chop is almost like a slice. Imagine that the ribbon is now a rope. It is at waist height. Make your hands into cups. Raise them just as you did to slice. Chop downward until the rope stops your hands. Your hands should pull back with a slight snap!

To do a *two-hand slice*, start with your arms straight down at your sides. Bend your elbows and slice upward with both hands. Quickly slice back downward. Now straighten your elbows. Slice using the full length of your arms. Start the same way for the *right-left slice*. Keep your left arm down and slice up with your right. Then slice down with your right and up with your left at the same time. Straighten your arms and slice right-left with your arms full length.

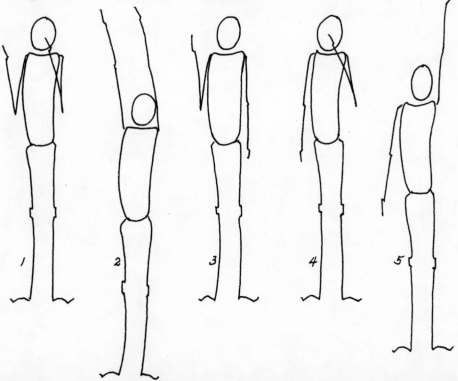

1   2   3   4   5

Practice both slices to a count of one-two. Each number is one beat. You should always do one movement for each beat in a cheer. First, do the two-hand slice. On one, raise both hands. On two, lower both hands. Now do the right-left slice. On one, raise your right hand. On two, lower your right hand and raise your left hand. Make your hands into cups and do the same movements with chops. Many movements can be done either way. Both chops and slices should always be done quickly.

Here is a *front-and-back chop*. Do it in four beats. Your count is one-two-three-four. To begin, cup your hands, palms facing forward. On beat one, raise both arms straight out to your sides, shoulder high. Two, bend your elbows. Raise your hands straight up and in toward your head. Bring your right hand down in front of your face. Bring your left hand down behind your head. Keep your elbows straight out to your sides. Three, straighten your arms. This brings both hands up and out to the sides again. On four, do the same movement you did on beat two. But this time lower your left hand in front of your face. Lower your right hand behind your head.

THRUSTS AND PUNCHES: Thrusts and punches are also similar to each other. To thrust, use more follow-through. To punch, pull back slightly. Use fists with both movements. You can thrust or punch your fists in any direction.

Stand with your feet together and your arms at your sides. Bend your elbows. Keep them close to your body. Raise your fists up to your shoulders. On beat one, thrust both fists straight out in front of you. Use the whole length of your arm. Snap your elbows. On beat two, bring your fists back to your shoulders. Now thrust your fists straight up above your shoulders. Bring them back down. Thrust straight out to your sides at shoulder height. Return to starting position. Thrust to the sides and down.

Here is a *side-to-side thrust.* Start with your fists at your shoulders. Keep the top of your left arm close to your side. Drop your left fist down across your waist. Do not straighten your elbow. On the same beat, thrust your right fist out to your right. Straighten your whole arm. Your right hand should be slightly higher than your shoulder. On the next beat, do the same motions in reverse. Thrust your right arm across your waist. Thrust your left arm to the left. Move both arms in and out quickly. Use a one-two count. Remember to snap your elbows!

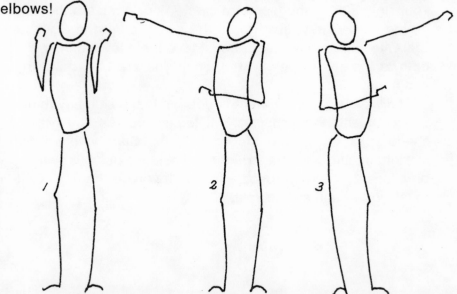

1   2   3

BE CREATIVE

You have now learned a lot of ideas about how to use your hands and arms. They will help you build cheers. But remember—cheerleading is creative! Do not be afraid to put together movements your own way. Learn the basics. Then use your imagination to build on them. The *windmill* is a movement that breaks the rules. You use sweeping arm movements. But your hands are in the fist position. Why? Someone liked it better that way. Here is how you do it.

Stand with your feet together, your right side toward the crowd. Hold your right arm straight out in front of you, waist high. Hold your left arm straight up above your left shoulder. Notice how far apart your hands are. They must stay the same distance apart while you move your arms. Now imagine that your right side is the face of a clock. Your arms are the hands on the clock. They must go all the way around the clock face. Start moving both arms at once. Move them toward your back, both at the same speed. Stop when you are back to starting position.

At first your arms will want to flop out to the sides. With practice your shoulder muscles will loosen up. As you practice, shape your hands into blades or fans. Start with one arm straight up and one arm straight down. Make up your own combinations. Invite other people to watch you do them. Ask them to tell you what they like best.

FOOTWORK

Footwork is like dancing. You just move your feet to the beat. Sometimes you will use a single step for each beat in a line. At other times you will use combination steps like swaying and rocking. Each sway or rock uses four beats.

To *sway*, start with your feet together. Step to the right with your right foot. Place your left foot beside your right foot. Step to the left with your left foot. Place your right foot next to your left. Sway to a count of four. Each step is one beat. As you begin a step, bend your knees slightly. Straighten them as you finish the step. The swaying comes from your knee action.

To *rock*, again stand with your feet together. With your toes pointed, step forward and to the right. Your toes will hit the ground first. As your right heel comes down, raise your left heel. On beat two, rock back onto your left heel. Your right heel lifts off the ground and your right toes are pointed. On beat three, step back on your right foot. Your toes should land first, then your heel. As your right heel comes down, your left heel lifts up. On the fourth beat, leave both feet where they are. Set your left heel down. Your right heel lifts up. Now step forward on your right foot and repeat the steps.

Stomps and hops are used to emphasize certain words. A *stomp* is just a stomp. Pick up one foot. Bring it down hard and flat. Stomp when you want to make noise. A *hop* is also just what it sounds like. With both feet together, bend your knees. Snap them straight and push off with your toes. In *backward hops*, your feet slide backward without leaving the ground. Bend your knees. Snap them straight and pull your feet back.

Here are some single steps to mix and match. Use them when you want a different step for each beat. Create combinations that *you* like. Always start with your feet together. Practice to a count of one-two-three-four. Do one-two with your right foot. On three-four, repeat the same step with your left foot.

On beat one, step to the side on your right foot. On beat two, return to starting position. You can also step in place. Bend your knee. Raise it high and point your toes. Step down on beat two. Now step back on your right foot. Bend your knee and put your foot flat on the ground. Keep your left leg straight with toes pointed. That is beat one. Return to starting position on beat two.

The lunge, the swing, and the twist are also single steps. To *lunge*, step forward and to the right on your right foot. Bend your right knee. Your weight will shift forward. Be sure to keep your back and your left leg straight. *Swing* your right foot across in front of your left leg. Return to starting position. Swing your left leg. To *twist*, keep your knees together and bend them slightly. As they bend, twist both knees to the right. Straighten your knees and twist to the left.

Now you have learned hand positions, arm movements, and footwork. You are ready to start building yells!

Chapter 5:
Yells

Yells are made up of arm movements, footwork, and words. Each yell must have a rhythm. The rhythm is made up of beats. Clap twice and say "o-kay." That is two beats. You did a movement and part of a word on each beat. You build yells by combining words and movements beat by beat.

First, find a rhythm. You can fit the words of a yell to the rhythm of a song. Or you can work out your own rhythm with claps and snaps. Next you must decide what happens on each beat. In the example above, you say "o" and clap on beat one. On beat two, you say "kay" and clap. In cheerleaders' code, it is written like this.

oX—kayX

say "o"   clap   pause   say "kay"   clap

The code lets you write down a yell beat by beat. It shows how the words and movements go together. To use it, you must learn a few more rules!

First, the code can tell you how to say a word. Hyphens between letters tell you to say each letter. When there are no hyphens, say the whole word.

o-k-a-y   Say each letter.
okay   Say the word.

The code uses symbols. A *symbol* is a letter that stands for a movement. "X" stands for clap. "—"stands for pause. XX—XX means clap twice, pause, clap twice. These two symbols always stand for claps and pauses. Other symbols stand for different movements in different yells.

When an X comes right after a word, clap at the same time you say the word. If there is a space between the X and the word, clap *after* you say the word.

okay X—XX   Say "okay" and clap. Pause. Clap twice.
okay X—XX   Say "okay." Then clap. Pause. Clap twice.

Now look underneath the word. When there is a space after the word, an arm movement may go there.

okay X—XX
T

"T" means thrust both arms out to your sides. The code tells you to say "okay" and thrust at the same time. Then clap, pause, clap twice. Sometimes you must do footwork and arm movements at the same time. Then it looks like this:

okay X—XX
T
O

"T" still means thrust. "O" stands for hop. Now you say "okay," thrust, and hop all at once.

Here is a school name yell. It uses words, hops, and claps. The words are the initials of a school. Use the initials of your own school. Without code, the yell looks like this:

SRHS
SRHS
SRHS

It doesn't tell you very much, does it? Here is the first line with movements. "O" stands for hop.

SX—XX RX—XX HX—XX SX—XX
O   O   O   O

Do the first line. Yell "S." At the same time, clap and hop. Pause, clap twice. Do R, H, and S the same way. The second line goes faster.

SX—RX—HX—SX
O   O   O   O

Yell the letter. Clap and hop as you yell it. Pause, yell the next letter. The last line is even faster.

SXRXHXSX
O O O O

Yell each letter as you hop and clap. Do not pause at all! Here is another yell:

LET'S GO

L-E-T
Apostrophe
S-G-O
Let's go, let's go

"Let's Go" uses three different arm movements. "A" stands for inside-out sweep. "B" stands for right-left slice. "C" stands for apostrophe. An apostrophe looks like a backward C. Draw it in the air with your right hand.

XXL-E-T XXXapostrophe XXXS-G-O Let's go, let's go
A   C   A   B   B

First, do just the arm movements. Clap twice. Inside-out sweep. Clap three times. Draw a backward C. Clap three times. Inside-out sweep. Right-left slice. Right-left slice. When you know the arm movements, yell the words along with them. Repeat the whole yell three times. The last time, say "let's go" three times. Now here is another yell.

COME ON BACK

One, two—three, four—five
T-H-S is ready to fight,
Six, seven—eight, nine—ten
Come on back and do it again!

"O" stands for step forward. "H" means hop backward. Do these movements to the first and third lines.

OneXtwoX—threeXfourX—fiveX
O   O   O   O   O

SixXsevenX—eightXnineX—tenX
H   H   H   H   H

Make up movements for the second and fourth lines. Put your imagination to work! Go ahead and do the rest of these yells and chants.

DEFEAT

The Trojans are the team
We're going to defeat,
So, come on everyone,
Do the Bulldog beat!
X—X—XX—X
O O OO O

The last line of this yell is claps and stomps. The clapping rhythm works for all the words. Here is the first line with claps.

TheX TroX jansXareX theXteam

Change the claps to footwork and arm movements. Choose motions that act out the words. Most yells are repeated at least three times.

WATCH OUT

We're the Tigers,
You'd better watch out
X—XX—XX
We're the team
You're worried about.
X—XX—XX
We've got might
X—XX
We've got spirit
X—XX
And we're going to fight.
X—XX—XX
We're the Tigers, so you better watch out!

GO, FIGHT, WIN

Go,
Let's do it,
Let's go for the Wildcats team!
Fight,
Let's do it,
Let's fight for the Wildcats team!
Win,
Let's do it,
Let's win for the Wildcats team!

HELLO

Taylor High School would like to say,
Hello to you in every way.
With pep and spirit,
We're ready to cheer.

Hey, hey, Badgers,
Good through the year.

GET DOWN

Get down—get going—get loose,
Move to the beat,
Get your whole body moving.
Let's start with your feet,
Everybody now,
Feet, two, three, four
Knees, two, three, four
Hips, two, three, four
Arms, two, three, four
Shoulders, two, three, four.

Get the crowd to do this yell with you. Yell "Feet" loud; then stomp on "two, three, four." Make up movements for knees, hips, arms, and shoulders.

CHANTS

Here are four chants for any occasion. All chants should be repeated at least three times. The first chant below works best when it is repeated five or six times. Yell the words louder each time.

We're from Denver, couldn't be prouder,
If you can't hear us now, we'll yell a little louder.

Hey, let's fire up,
Say, hey, let's fire up.

Oakland—can you say it?
Everyone's here, so everyone cheer!

We areXX—the WarriorsXX

Yell the following five chants when the other team has the ball.

> Defense attack, get that ball back!

> T-a k-e, let's take that ball away.

> No, no, not that way,
> Take that ball the other way.

> Everyone—take someone,
> Don't let 'em go.

> Grab it, steal it, take it away!

And, last, here are five offensive chants. Yell them when your team has the ball.

> Go, go, get 'em, get 'em,
> Go, get 'em, go!

> We want a touchdown so-o-o bad.

> We want two from you,
> Say, we want two from you.

> Set it up, put it in,
> That's the way we're going to win.

> Dribble it, pass it, we want a basket!

Chapter 6:
Jumps

Jumps are the fireworks of cheerleading. They are fun for the cheerleaders and the crowd. Use them in any part of a cheer. When you begin, jump to draw the crowd's attention. During the yell, jump to emphasize the most important word. At the end of a yell, use jumps to boost spirit.

Be careful not to use up all your fireworks at once. The crowd will get bored with too many jumps, and you will be worn out before the game is half over. Jump only at the highest points of the cheer.

When you do use jumps, vary them often. Make them high and graceful. To jump high, you must use both your legs and arms. Lift with your arms and spring with your legs. Practice jumping high as you learn the straight jump. Later you will learn posed jumps.

STRAIGHT JUMP

Stand straight, arms at your sides. Step forward on your right foot. As you step, swing your arms up and out to your sides. Step forward on your left foot. Bend forward and cross your arms in front. Hop and swing your arms back. As you end the hop, swing your arms forward, then up. Push off with your feet as your arms swing upward. At the top of the jump, hold your head and body still. This will make your jump look higher. Land on your toes with your feet together. Bend your knees and dig in your heels. Stretch out your arms for balance.

Vary the straight jump by moving your arms into different positions. At the top of the jump, thrust your arms above your head. Thrust them to the sides. Cross them in front of your shoulders. Pay attention to form as you jump. Point your toes. Arch your back and hold your shoulders level. Keep your arms straight and your fingers together. Remember to look at the crowd. Smile!

POSED JUMPS

Here are six posed jumps. Stand still and practice the poses. Then move into the pose at the top of your jump.

Stag Leap

Jump with your left side toward the crowd. As you reach the top of the jump, place your left hand on your hip. Fling your right fist over your head. Point your toes and bend both knees. Place your right leg slightly forward. Bend your left leg back slightly.

Spread Eagle

Jump facing the crowd. Spread your feet wide. Thrust both arms straight up above your shoulders. Point your toes and fingers. Then try these variations. Hold your arms out to your sides, shoulder high. Lower them until your hands are at waist level. Drop them straight down, fingers pointing at the ground.

Fight Leap

Fling your left arm out to your side. Thrust your right fist upward. Bend your right elbow. Spread your feet wide apart. Bend your right knee.

Side Banana

Jump facing the crowd. Arch your body to the right. Keep your feet together, toes pointed. Try to look like a banana! Put your right fist on your hip. Curve your left arm and thrust your fist over your head.

Squat

Cross your arms. Point your right-hand fingers toward your left shoulder. Point your left-hand fingers toward your right shoulder. Bend your legs and pull your knees up and forward. Draw up both feet as high as you can. Keep your legs together. Make sure that your back is straight and your shoulders are level.

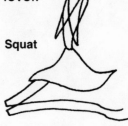

Squat

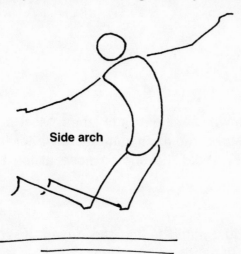

Side arch

Side Arch

Jump facing the crowd. Arch your body to the left. Fling your fists out to the sides. With your legs a few inches apart, bend your knees. Keep your feet together and point your toes.

LANDINGS

A graceful landing is part of a good jump. Before you jump, decide how you will land. To make jumps look higher, land in a low position. Crouch with your knees together, or with one foot ahead of the other. For snappy landings, land in a lunge position, or on one foot. As soon as both feet hit the ground, go into an ending.

Chapter 7:
Endings

An *ending* tells the crowd the cheer is finished. Most endings are *poses* or *freezes*. Move into them immediately after the last word of the yell. Always hold the ending pose at least three seconds.

BASIC POSE

For a simple ending, just stand facing the crowd. Keep your feet together. Place both hands on your hips.

STRADDLE FREEZE

You can do the Straddle Freeze with four different arm positions. Hop and land with your feet wide apart. Thrust both arms straight up above your shoulders. Now here are some variations. Thrust your right arm upward; place your left hand on your hip. Or thrust your right arm up, and point your left arm straight down. Finally, fling both arms out to your sides, shoulder high. By changing your arm positions, you can use the Straddle Freeze often.

SIDE FREEZE

To do this freeze, stand with your left side toward the crowd. Lunge forward on your right foot. Thrust your right arm up and forward. Place your left arm down and back. Line it up with your left leg.

CUTOFF

Start the Cutoff with your hands together over your head. Keep your arms straight. Slice sharply down and out to your sides. As you slice, step forward with your right foot. Bend your right knee. Drop your left knee to the ground.

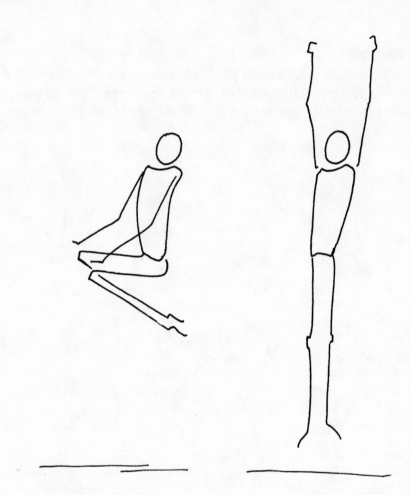

KNEE SLAP

The Knee Slap combines a jump and a pose. Start with a straight jump. At the top of the jump, draw your knees forward and up. Slap your knees with both hands. To land, thrust your arms over your head. Drop your feet straight down. As you hit the ground, keep your arms up and your feet together. Hold this pose for a few seconds.

Now you have learned the parts that make up most cheers. Find new ways to put them together. Make up new movements. Watch other cheerleaders and learn their movements. Cheer-leading is always growing and changing. Go along with it. But keep your enthusiastic personality! It will always be the most important part of cheerleading.

PART II
BATON TWIRLING

Chapter 8:
Patience and Practice

The baton flashes and sparkles—side to side, overhead, under the leg. It looks as if the twirler's hands are going a hundred miles a minute. But nobody can move that fast. That is the magic of baton twirling! The speed is an illusion. You do not have to be faster than the speed of light to make it happen.

You do have to be patient. Twirls are made up of small, exact motions. To move the baton quickly through many different motions, you must practice often. At first your wrists will tire very quickly. At times you may feel clumsy and frustrated. Maybe you will even think you can never get it right. But the more you practice, the easier twirling becomes. One day you will see your baton spin with sparkle and ease. Your wrist muscles will finally begin to cooperate. Your free hand will stay on your hip without being reminded. The basic twirls will become second nature. With patience and practice, you can learn to do magic.

Chapter 9:
Before You Start

WHAT TO WEAR

When you twirl, you will use your arms, legs, and body. The baton must spin very close to you. Sometimes it will pass under your leg or between your arm and body. Twirling costumes *must* allow both you and the baton to move freely. For practice, it is best to wear leotards or shorts and T-shirts. Shorts and shirts should fit close to your body. Avoid wide sleeves or cuffs that get in your way. When you start out, wear lightweight shoes. High steps and leg raises tire your feet and legs quickly. Tennis shoes or ballet slippers will keep your feet light and flexible.

YOUR BATON

The metal part of a baton is called the *shaft*. On one end of the shaft, there is a round, rubber *ball*. On the other end, there is a rubber *tip*. When you buy your baton, make sure the shaft is the right length for your arm. Also, choose a baton that has good weight and balance.

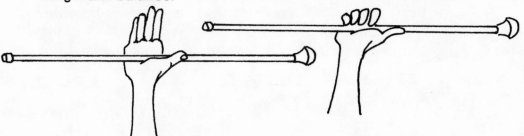

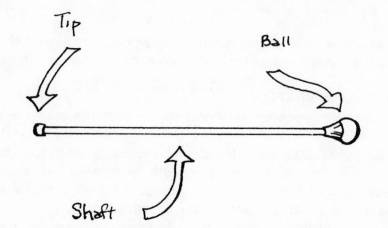

Many music stores fit and order batons. To find your size, measure from high under your arm to the ends of your fingers. Then try a baton that length. Straighten your arm and curl your fingers. Rest the ball of the baton on your curled fingers. If the length is correct, the tip should just fit under your arm.

Batons are usually made in even-numbered lengths. If your arm is an odd number of inches long, you will not find an exact fit. In that case, it is better to buy a baton slightly longer than your arm. For example, if your arm is 19 inches (48 cm) long, you will need a 20-inch (51-cm) baton. Baton shafts also vary in weight and thickness. Thin, lightweight batons are less tiring for beginners.

A baton is not as demanding as a puppy, but it does need some attention. Unless you are a wizard, the ball and tip will get dirty. You can clean them with warm, soapy water. Wash them often so they will not turn gray and grubby. To avoid loosening the ball and tip, never pull them off the shaft. Even with good care, rubber baton parts usually do not last as long as the shaft. If the ball and tip wear out, order new ones at the store where you bought your baton. The baton shaft needs very little care. Store it in a safe place so it will not get bent or dented. Its finish should stay shiny without much help from you. But to give it extra sparkle, shine it with silver polish now and then.

GETTING IN SHAPE

In baton work, posture and graceful movements are as important as quick wrists. You have probably noticed the twirler's light, high-arched step. Head and shoulders seem to float in the air. Every motion looks smooth and easy. The twirler's grace comes from exercise and practice. You must make exercise a regular part of your twirling practice.

Rocking strengthens your back and stomach muscles. Lie on your stomach. Bend your knees and point your toes toward your head. Put your palms on the floor beside your waist. Tip your head back and lift your chest off the floor. Now your body is arched like the base of a rocking chair. To rock backward, push on the floor with your palms. Your chest will lift up as your knees go down. To rock forward, stop pushing with your hands. Let your elbows bend. Your chest will come down as your knees lift up.

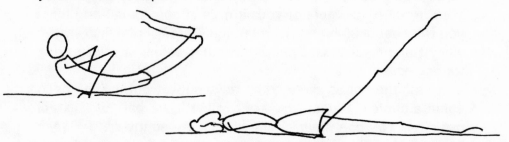

Leg lifts build your arches and strengthen your legs. This time lie on your back with your legs together. Keep both legs straight and stiff. Arch your feet and point your toes. Slowly lift, then lower, your right leg. Then lift and lower your left leg. Lift each leg as high as you can without bending your knees.

Waist stretches limber and strengthen the muscles in your upper body. Kneel with your legs together. Raise both arms straight up above your head. Keep your arms stretched overhead as you lean slowly to the side. Slowly straighten until you are back in starting position. Then lean to the other side and straighten.

The *peek* is good for arches, ankles, and back and stomach muscles. Lie on your back, arms at your sides. Arch your feet and point your toes to the floor. Keep your legs straight. Only your head and feet will move. Bend your ankles and point your toes to your head. Raise your head and look at your toes. Peek! Count to three. Lower your head and feet to starting position. Peek again.

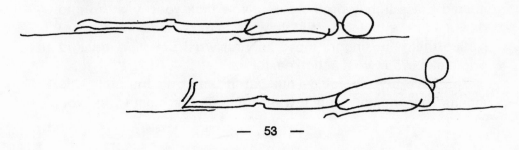

Chapter 10: Three Basic Twirls

The spin of the baton comes from wrist action. At first your wrists will probably feel stiff and clumsy. With practice your muscles will limber up. But until they do, your wrists and hands will tire quickly. When one hand gets tired, give it a break. You must learn to twirl just as smoothly with one hand as the other. So let your right and left hands take turns resting on your hip.

Although your wrists do the real work, your fingers can help them. A firm, easy grip is important. First, hold out your right hand, palm up and open. Point the ball of the baton in the same direction as your thumb. Place the center of the shaft on your palm. Let the flat of your thumb rest against the shaft. Curl all four fingers loosely around the shaft. Now you are holding the baton *thumb to the ball*.

To test your grip, drop your arm straight down to your side. The baton should rest on your curved fingers. Your thumb should press lightly on the shaft. Now flick your wrist up and down, back and forth. Watch your fingers—and your nose! Notice that your fingers move as your wrist bends. A relaxed grip makes your wrist action easier.

You have been holding your baton thumb to the ball. This means your thumb points toward the ball. For most twirls, you will grip the baton in this position. However, not all baton work is twirling. Sometimes you will hold the baton *thumb to the tip*. But as a rule, use the thumb to the ball position. Most baton work is also done with the *ball leading.* This means that the ball of the baton goes first. Now you are ready to twirl!

PINWHEEL
In the Pinwheel, the baton twirls in a front-to-back direction. The ball points front, down, back, and up. To start, take the baton in your right hand, thumb to the ball.

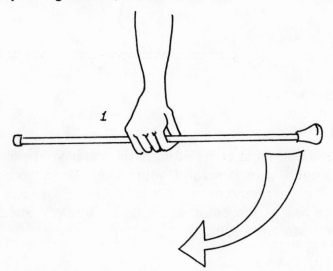

Let your right arm hang loosely at your right side. The ball of the baton points forward. The tip points back. Dip your wrist forward until the ball points straight to the ground. The tip now points upward along the outside of your arm. Continue to turn your wrist until your palm faces slightly upward and to the outside. Your arm has turned inside-out. The ball now points straight back.

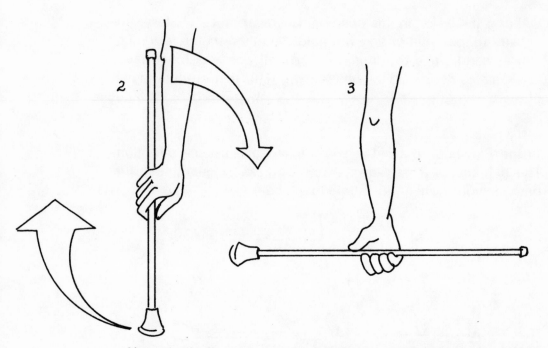

Next the ball must come straight up under your arm. It will pass between your arm and your body. Bend your elbow slightly. Flip your hand over. Your palm now faces toward your body. The ball of the baton again points straight ahead. You are back to starting position.

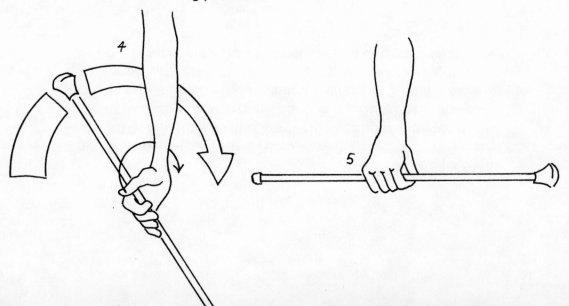

Work through the Pinwheel slowly. Do one step at a time until you understand how the baton should move. Then forget about the steps. Relax your fingers and spin in one continuous motion. As you twirl Pinwheels, the ball of the baton should always pass under your arm. The tip should always pass outside your arm. As the ball passes under your arm, your elbow must bend slightly. At all other times, it should be straight. At first, though, you probably will find that your elbow wobbles every which way. For right now, the wobbles are okay. Work on holding the baton with a firm, easy grip. Let it move in your fingers as you turn your wrist. Watch out for the ball as it passes under your arm. Try to keep it from hitting you! As your wrists limber up, your elbow will straighten itself out. Practice is the only way to make it happen.

As you learn the basic twirls, practice good posture, too. Always stand with your feet almost together. Pull up your chin and shoulders. Keep your back straight and your stomach pulled in. Remind your free hand that it belongs on your hip. Also remember that both hands have to learn the same twirls. When one hand gets tired, give it a rest. Put the other hand to work for a few spins. Now if you have untangled yourself from the Pinwheel, try the Flat.

FLAT
In the Flat, the baton spins from side to side. The ball points right, back, left, and front. Pick up the baton in your right hand, thumb to the ball.

Hold your arm straight out to your right side, at shoulder height. Straighten your wrist. Your palm faces down. The baton tip points straight along the underside of your arm, toward your body. Bend your wrist backward. Now your palm faces out to the side. The ball points straight back. The tip points straight ahead. Bend your elbow slightly. Turn your hand toward your body. The ball now points at your head. Continue to turn your hand until the ball points straight to the front. Your palm should now face out to the side again. Roll your hand to the outside. At the same time, straighten your wrist and elbow. Your palm will turn down, and then forward. As it turns, the tip of the baton will pass under your arm.

As the tip passes under your arm, your wrist and elbow must be straight. Otherwise, the baton may bruise your arm. Remember to keep your body straight as you practice. Do not lean toward your baton. To do the Flat correctly, you also must keep your arm at shoulder height. This position is very tiring. When your arm begins to droop, change hands immediately. A drooping Flat can quickly become a bad habit! It is easier to learn it right than to change the habit later. Be patient. Your arm muscles will appreciate it.

FIGURE 8

Here it is—the last basic twirl! Grasp the baton in your right hand, thumb to the ball. Hold the shaft flat in front of you at waist height. The ball points left; the tip points right. Now imagine a lazy 8 lying on its side. You are going to draw the 8 with the ball of your baton.

To start, dip the ball down to the left. Then flip your hand over to the right. Your palm faces up. The ball points slightly forward and down to the right. Bend your hand back. The tip will now point slightly forward and up to the left. Flip your hand over so your palm faces down. The tip and the ball reverse their positions. Flick your wrist toward your body to return the ball to starting position.

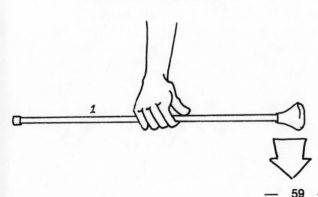

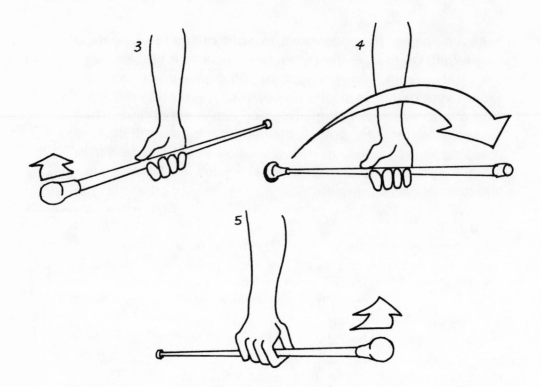

Now repeat the Figure 8. Round out the curves while keeping your arm as straight as you can. Relax your hand and twirl faster. Let the shaft rotate between your thumb and first finger. Guide the baton with your other fingers. As you gain speed, each loop of the Figure 8 becomes a twirl. Watch out for your chin and elbows!

COMBINATIONS

A *combination* is made up of two or more twirls. You must change from twirl to twirl without stopping your wrist action. As soon as you can spin steadily through each twirl, start practicing combinations.

First, combine Pinwheels with Flats. Spin eight Pinwheels at your right side. As you finish the last Pinwheel, raise your arm to shoulder height. Spin eight Flats. Change hands and repeat the combination. At first you may lose your rhythm as you shift from Pinwheels to Flats. When you can make the change smoothly, do it sooner. Spin four Pinwheels, then four Flats. Combine the basic twirls every way you can imagine. Go from Pinwheels to Figure 8s and back to Pinwheels. Combine Flats with Figure 8s. Do all three twirls, one after the other. Combinations are the beginning of more complicated routines.

Chapter II:
Variations

The three basic twirls can also be done with *variations*. Each variation uses only one twirl. The baton is moved into different positions as it spins. This means your wrist must do one thing while the rest of you does something else!

FRONT-TO-BACK PINWHEEL

With your right arm at your side, start doing Pinwheels. When your baton is spinning evenly, begin the arm movements. First, raise your right arm straight forward. When your hand is waist high, stop and count off four twirls. Sill twirling, return your arm to starting position. Count four twirls. Next move your arm straight back. Stop and count four twirls. Last, return to starting position for another count of four. Now do the Front-to-Back with your left hand.

SIDE-TO-SIDE FLAT

The Side-to-Side must be done with your arm straight and at shoulder height. At first it is even more tiring than spinning Flats. Change hands often. Do not let your arm get tired enough to droop.

   Begin with your right arm straight out to your side, shoulder high. Start spinning Flats. Move your arm forward. Center it in front of your body. Count off four spins. Then twist your waist to the left. Bring your right arm across your body. The baton should now be out to your left side. Count four twirls. Untwist your waist. Return your arm to the front, center position. Twirl four more Flats. Finally, return to starting position and do four twirls. Keep your baton spinning steadily as you change arm positions. Move slowly from one position to the next. Twirl four times in each position.

TWO-HAND FIGURE 8

Stand straight and put your left hand on your hip. With your right hand in front of you, twirl four Figure 8s. The fifth time the ball dips to the left, change hands. Take the baton in your left hand, thumb to the ball. Place your right hand on your hip. Twirl four Figure 8s with your left hand. On the fifth dip to the right, return the baton to your right hand. Put your left hand back on your hip. Keep twirling as you change hands. Always grasp the baton thumb to the ball.

Practice starting off with both your right and your left hand. Then practice changing hands on the second twirl. Now here is another Pinwheel variation.

UP-AND-DOWN PINWHEEL

Twirl steadily as you move your arm through these six positions. One, twirl Pinwheels at your right side. Two, slowly raise your right arm until it is straight above your shoulder. Three, lower your hand to waist level. Keep it straight out to the front. Four, bend forward. Bring your hand down beside your right knee. Five, straighten your body and return your arm to waist level. Six, return your arm to starting position. Move through the up and down positions without stopping. Keep your twirling arm straight. Raise and lower it slowly and steadily. Twirl all the time your arm is moving. Remember to rest your free hand on your hip. Keep your body straight. Do not lean to the side when you bend forward.

UNDER LEG FIGURE 8
Before you work through this variation, practice the legwork. Stand straight with your feet a few inches apart. Bend your right knee and raise it high. Point your toes to the ground. Keep your left leg straight. It must not bend even slightly. Now set your right foot down. Quickly raise your left knee as you did your right. As you raise each knee, you will pass the baton under your leg.

Begin the Figure 8 with your right hand. As the ball dips to start the third twirl, raise your right knee. Drop your right arm. Pass the baton under your leg, ball leading. With your left hand palm up, grasp the center of the shaft. Lower your right leg. Straighten your body. Spin two Figure 8s with your left hand. As the ball dips for the third spin, raise your left knee. Drop your left arm. Pass the baton under your left leg, ball leading. Grasp the center of the shaft with the palm of your right hand. Set your left foot down. Twirl two Figure 8s with your right hand. Always grasp the baton thumb to the ball. Pass it under your leg quickly. Change hands without a break in rhythm. Continue to twirl as you lower your foot to the ground.

Do not hunch forward as you pass the baton under your leg. Keep your shoulders level and drop your arm low. As you raise one leg, the other knee may want to bend. Tell it to stiffen up! While doing any variation, pay special attention to posture and form. Some movements can leave you bent or twisted every which way. Remember to straighten yourself out after each movement.

FRONT-TO-BACK PINWHEEL

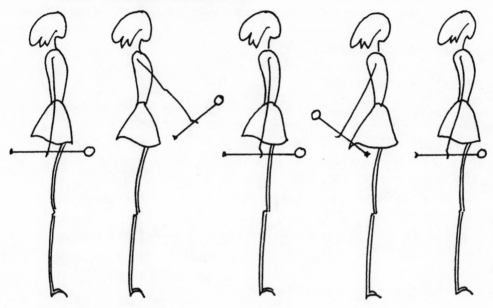

SIDE-TO-SIDE FLAT

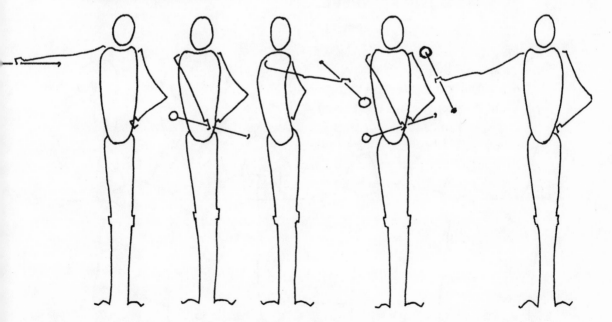

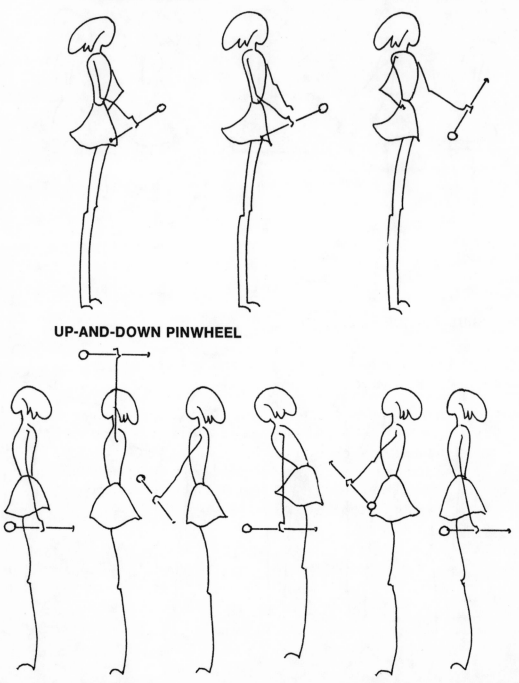

TWO-HAND FIGURE 8

UP-AND-DOWN PINWHEEL

UNDER LEG FIGURE 8

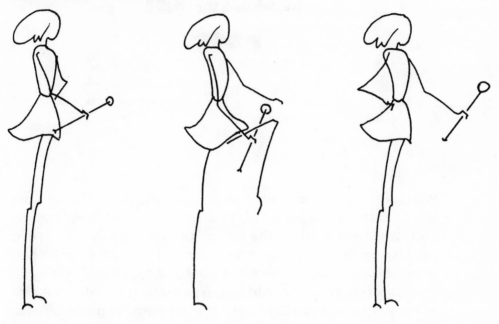

Now you have learned combinations and variations. Try putting them together in different ways. Then make up some of your own. The basic rules of baton work give you a good start. But you also must learn to use the rules creatively. Learn the basics and then use them as building blocks. Practice in front of a mirror as you make up routines. Decide what looks good to you. Put your personality into your baton work!

Chapter 12: Poses

Poses add variety and style to your baton work. You can use them several different ways. In a routine, move from pose to pose while you twirl. At the end of a routine, go into a pose as you stop twirling. In group work, pose while another twirler performs. Always hold a pose for at least one count.

Most poses are done with your free arm extended to the side or back. Practice posing your hand and arm in graceful positions. Keep your fingers straight and close together. Point them outward. Point your thumb downward. Your thumb and fingers should form a V shape. In this position your free hand is ready to grasp the baton.

UP ON TOES
Go up on your toes as you turn from side to side in a routine. Just bring your feet together and stand on your toes. From this position, you can go straight into another pose.

LUNGE
Start twirling with your right hand. Go up on your toes and pivot to the right. Step forward on your right foot. Bend your right knee and shift your weight forward. Keep your left leg

straight behind you. Your left foot stays on the ground, toes pointing slightly to the left. As you lunge, keep twirling. Extend your left arm out to your side. Keep your right arm straight.

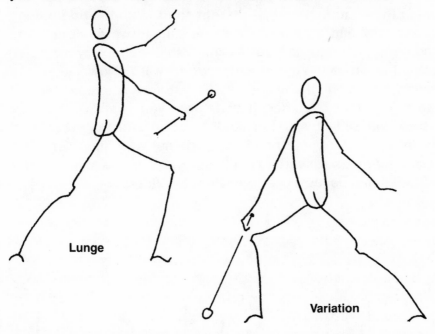

Lunge

Variation

Now try a variation. Twirl Pinwheels with your right hand. As the ball spins to the front, toss the baton forward slightly. Let the shaft slide along your fingers. Grasp it near the tip. As you catch the baton, lunge forward on your right foot. Straighten your right arm. Touch the ball of the baton to the ground in front of your right toes. Your arm and your baton should form a straight line. Pose your left arm out to the side. Hold the pose for a count of one. Then return your feet to starting position. Swing the ball of the baton toward your left hand. Grasp the center of the shaft, thumb to the ball. Twirl with your left hand.

SALUTE

Use a Salute between twirls or to begin a routine. Start with your feet together and your left arm at your side. Grasp the baton thumb to the tip in your right hand. With the tip pointing upward, extend your right arm up and forward. Your hand should be as high as your head. With a bend of your wrist, point the tip left. Your palm faces forward. Now imagine a hollow tube along the inside of your left arm. The tube starts at the top of your shoulder. It ends near your waist. Bend your elbow and slide the baton straight down into the tube. Stop when the back of your hand rests against your shoulder. Your palm still faces forward. Your thumb points down. Your right elbow should be level with your right shoulder.

ARABESQUE

Twirl steadily with your right hand as you do the Arabesque. Pose your free hand out to the side. Lock your knee to keep your right leg straight. Lean forward slightly and raise your left leg behind you. Do not bend your left knee. Arch your foot and point your toes. Raise your leg as high as you can. Hold the pose for at least one count.

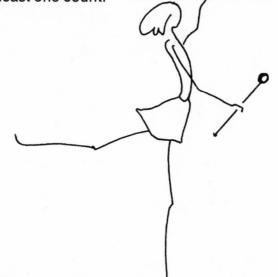

WAIST POSE

Place your left hand on your hip. Twirl eight Flats with your right hand. End the eighth twirl with the ball pointing left. Now you must make three moves all at once! First, raise your left arm straight up above your shoulder. Keep your fingers straight and together. Face your palm to the right. Second, lower your right arm to waist level. Bend your elbow and bring your forearm across your waist. Hold the baton at your left side, ball pointing straight back. The center of the shaft is beside your waist. Third, raise your left knee. Arch your left foot beside your right knee. Point your toes. Count one. Return to starting position. Twirl eight more Flats with your right hand.

As you pass the baton across your body, make sure your left arm is out of the way. When you raise your foot, hold it near your other knee. Do not let your foot and leg touch. Practice until you can go into the Waist Pose quickly. Use one count to get into position. Hold the pose for **one more count.**

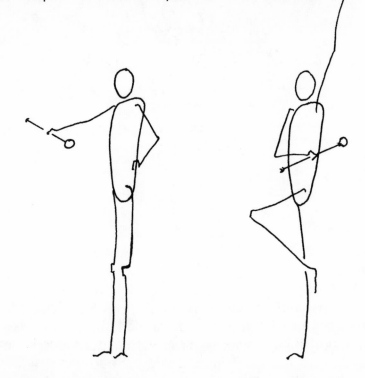

EXTENDED ARM POSE

Twirl Pinwheels with your right hand. On the eighth twirl, bring the baton tip inside your arm. As the tip comes up, raise your arm. Bend your elbow and flip your hand upward. The baton tip now points down behind your elbow. The ball points up and slightly forward. As you pose the baton, raise your left knee as you did in the Waist Pose. Position your left arm out to the side.

The same arm pose can be used as a *stationary* position. In stationaries, you pose only the baton. Your left hand stays on your hip. Unless you are marching, both feet remain on the ground.

UNDER ARM STATIONARY

Turn the back of your right hand up. Place your baton in the V between your thumb and first finger. Grip the shaft just below the ball with your thumb and finger. Curl your other three fingers underneath the shaft. Slide the lower end of the shaft between your waist and arm. The tip should point down and back. Hold the ball up in front of your right shoulder. Roll your wrist back and forth to a left-right beat.

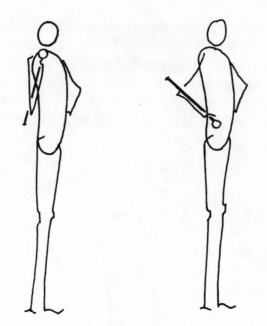

WAIST STATIONARY

Hold the baton as you did in the Under Arm Stationary. Rest the shaft along the outside of your arm. Place your palm against your waist on your right side. The baton shaft fits into the crease at your elbow. The tip points out to the side and back.

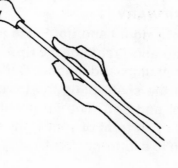

Chapter 13:
The Strut

The twirler's high, prancing step is called the Strut. It is as important in routines as it is in marching. Pull your shoulders back and prepare to strut. Hold your chin up. Straighten your back and flatten your stomach. Put your left hand on your hip. Hold the baton in your right hand. Pose it in the Waist Stationary position.

In march music, the drum beats left-right, left-right. You must always start out on your left foot. With your feet a few inches apart, raise your left knee. Point your toes and arch your foot. Bring your left toes up beside your right knee. Do not touch your left foot to your right leg. Keep your right leg very straight. Now step down on your left toes. Then set your heel down lightly. Lock your left knee. Raise your right knee to begin the next step.

As you strut, think "left-right, left-right." Practice holding your baton in the Waist and Under Arm Stationary positions. Move the ball of the baton left-right in time with your steps. When you can step smoothly and evenly, begin to twirl as you strut.

Chapter 14:
Fingers and the Flip

Now you have mastered strutting and wrist action. Your muscles do what they are told. The baton no longer thumps your elbows, nose, and shins. You can change twirls, hands, or positions smoothly. Surprise! Here is a twirl that uses fingers—and a flip that uses everything.

FINGERS

To grasp the baton, hold your right hand in front of you, palm facing up. Keep your first finger straight. Curl your other three fingers into your palm. Point the ball of the baton to your right. Place the center of the shaft across your first finger. Loop your finger and thumb around the shaft.

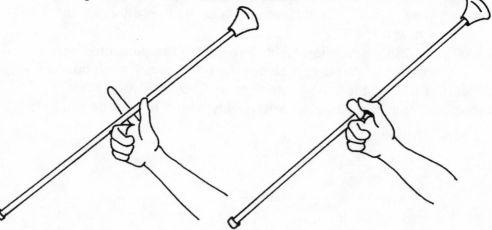

Now flick your wrist over so that the ball points left. As the baton flips over, straighten your second finger. Catch the shaft between your first and second fingers. Flick your wrist to the left again. This time, straighten your third finger to catch the shaft. The ball now points right again. Flick again and straighten your little finger. The ball points left. Do one more flick of your wrist. This time turn your hand over all the way. Your palm should face down. The baton shaft goes under your little finger and over your next three fingers. Straighten your little finger and let go of the baton. The shaft will roll across the backs of your fingers. Catch it between your thumb and first finger. Curl all four fingers around the shaft. Now you are holding the baton thumb to the ball. From this position you can go into any of the basic twirls.

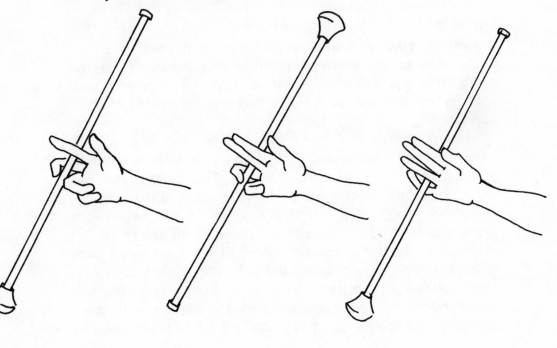

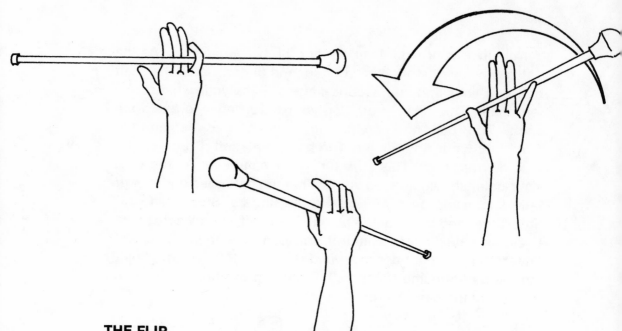

THE FLIP

A good Flip takes a lot of practice. You probably will drop your baton often as you learn to flip it. In fact the baton may go flying off in any direction. But it will soon begin to go where you send it. Until it does, though, give yourself plenty of practice space.

To begin, grasp your baton thumb to the ball in your right hand. Your palm faces down. The ball points to your left. Roll your wrist to the left, as far as it will go. Then quickly roll it as far as you can to the right. As your palm turns upward, straighten your fingers. Hold the shaft in the V between your thumb and first finger. The ball will swing down and to the left until the shaft catches on your thumb. It will then swing back down, to the right, and up. As the ball swings right, toss your hand upward. At the same time, flick your wrist to the left. Relax your thumb and let the shaft go. The baton will flip over, ball leading. Face the palm of your right hand forward, fingers pointing up. Grab the baton out of the air. Make sure you catch it thumb to the ball. You are now ready to go into a twirl!

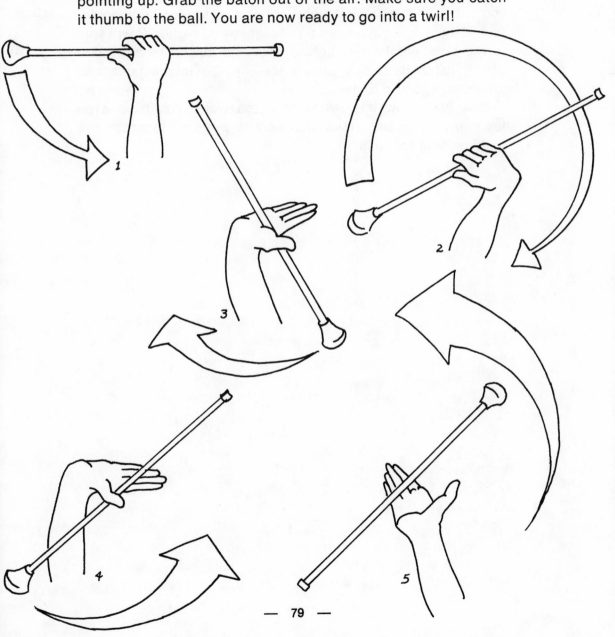

The motions leading up to the Flip must be done quickly. As you turn your wrist left-right-left, the baton gains momentum. With practice, you can flip it higher and higher. It will spin in the air several times before it comes down. As the baton drops, catch it quickly and gracefully. Go into a pose and immediately begin to twirl.

Now you know the basics of baton work. You have even learned two special tricks. It is time to put it all together and build twirling routines.

Chapter 15: Routines

Routines are made up of twirls, combinations, variations, and poses. You must combine these parts to create a pattern. Each movement in a routine should be done to a count. A *count* is just "one-two-three-four," and so on. It allows you to measure the parts of a routine. For example, do Pinwheels with your right hand for four counts. Then do Pinwheels with your left hand for four counts. Each count is like an inch on a ruler. You might do one movement for four inches, and another movement for one inch. Inches add up to feet, and counts add up to routines.

To get you started, here are some examples.

ROUTINE 1

Face forward. Twirl Figure 8s with your right hand for a count of four. Go up on your toes. Turn to the right. Twirl Up-and-Down Pinwheels for a count of twelve. Go up on your toes. Face forward. Twirl Figure 8s for a count of four. Change hands. Twirl Figure 8s with your left hand for four counts. Go up on your toes. Turn to the left. Twirl Up-and-Down Pinwheels for a count of twelve. Go up on your toes. Face forward. Twirl

Figure 8s for two counts. Change hands. Twirl Figure 8s for two more counts. End the routine in a Waist Pose. Hold the pose for two counts.

ROUTINE 2

Position your baton in the Salute Pose. Strut in place for a count of four. Flip the ball of the baton forward and do Figure 8s for eight counts. Twirl Side-to-Side Flats for sixteen counts. Lunge forward and touch the ball of the baton to the ground. Hold the pose for one count. Flip the ball to the left. Catch the shaft in your left hand. Twirl Front-and-Back Pinwheels for sixteen counts. Twirl Figure 8s for four counts. Change hands. Spin Pinwheels at your right side to a count of eight. Go into the Extended Arm Pose to end the routine.

ROUTINE 3

Do the Waist Pose for one count. Twirl Figure 8s for four counts. Pass the baton under your right leg. Twirl Figure 8s with your left hand for a count of four. Go up on toes. Turn to your right. Twirl Flats for eight counts. Go into the Arabesque Pose. Move your left arm to center, front position. Twirl Flats for eight more counts. Go up on your toes. Face forward, still spinning Flats. Take the baton in your right hand. Twirl Flats for eight counts. Flip the baton. Catch it with your right hand. Go up on your toes. Turn to the left. Twirl Up-and-Down Flats for sixteen counts. Go up on your toes. Face forward. Twirl Pinwheels at your right side for eight counts. End with a salute.

You can create many different routines by using the basics. Work out some routines of your own. Design them to emphasize your best twirls and poses. Find positions that turn your best side toward the audience. Routines are meant to show off your personality and talent. Do what works best for *you*.

There are still many more twirls, combinations, and poses that you can learn. By now you may have decided to go on to the next level of baton work. If you have, this is a good time to join a class or group. Before you go much further, you should learn to work to music. You also should learn to work with other twirlers. It is best to learn advanced twirling skills from an experienced teacher.

The Next Step

Both cheerleading and baton twirling are individual skills. But they are also social activities. Your skill and talent will grow much faster if you work with other people. For your next training step, you should join a class or group. In many cities, dance schools now teach both cheerleading and twirling. Your local YMCA or Parks and Recreation Department may also give lessons. And, official organizations hold camps, clinics, and competitions all over the country.

CHEERLEADING

The National Cheerleaders Association (NCA) sponsors summer camps. It offers clinics and workshops at high schools and colleges in the spring, summer, and fall. The International Cheerleading Foundation (ICF) also holds camps and workshops. Some of them are especially for beginners. Students are eleven through eighteen years old. You can also learn many cheers and advanced skills from official cheerleading handbooks. To learn the NCA's cheers read *Go! Fight! Win!* by Betty Lou Phillips. Look up the ICF's cheers in *The Official Cheerleader's Handbook* by Randy Neil. For more information on camps and clinics write to:

National Cheerleaders Association
9150 Markville
Dallas, Texas 75238

International Cheerleading Foundation
7800 Conser Place
Overland Park, Kansas 66204

BATON TWIRLING

The International Baton Twirling Association of America and Abroad conducts many activities for twirlers. It sponsors contests and gives awards and scholarships. It also publishes a magazine called "Let's Twirl." The World Federation of Baton Twirling and Majorette Associations promotes twirling for young people all over the world. These organizations can also tell you about twirling groups in your part of the country. Write to:

International Baton Twirling Association
of America and Abroad
Box 234
Waldwick, New Jersey 07463

World Federation of Baton Twirling
and Majorette Associations
P.O. Box 266
Janesville, Wisconsin 53545

TRYOUTS

Sooner or later, you probably will want to perform in front of a crowd. Members of cheerleading squads and twirling groups are often chosen by *trying out*. This means you must show your ability by performing in front of judges. The judges look for personality and skill. Many students try out, but only a few can be chosen. To be among those few you must display the qualities and skills required by the squad for which you try out.

To prepare for tryouts, first decide which group you want to join. Find out what requirements you must meet. Then watch the members of that group as they practice and perform. Ask them questions. Learn the cheers or routines they are doing. Then make up new ones of your own. Practice every day to build your skill and confidence.

When tryout day arrives, relax. Smile and let your personality take over. Good luck!

Index